On Hearing the Truth:

An Epistemology of the Ear

In a Postmodern World

By

Todd Speidell, Ph.D.

Wipf and Stock Publishers
Eugene, Oregon

ON HEARING THE TRUTH: AN EPISTEMOLOGY OF THE EAR IN A POSTMODERN WORLD

ISBN:1-59752-805-6

"If it sounds good, it is good."

ϕ Duke Ellington

Philosophy, religion, and science have always been closely related. The emphasis shifts, but the point is the same: the importance of ideas and understanding, of making sense out of our world and seeing our lives in some larger, even cosmic, perspective. Ideas define our place in the universe, our relations with other people; ideas determine what is important and what is not important, what is fair and what is not fair, what is worth believing and what is not worth believing. Ideas give life meaning. Our minds need ideas the way our bodies need food. We are starved for visions, hungry for understanding. We are caught up in the routines of life, distracted occasionally by the equally uninspired activities we call 'recreation' and 'entertainment.' What we as a nation have lost is the joy of thinking, the challenge of understanding, the inspirations as well as the consolations of philosophy.

Φ Robert Solomon

What is the meaning of human life, or organic life altogether? To answer this question at all implies a religion. Is there any sense then, you ask, in it? I answer, the man who regards his own life and that of his fellow-creatures as meaningless is not merely unfortunate but almost disqualified for life.

Φ Albert Einstein

Preface to the Reader

As you have noticed by the title, this book has something to do with language, meaning, and truth. Nevertheless, titles and covers are always somewhat misleading, and there are multiple clichés advising us against judging them too quickly. This book does not attempt simply to speak about or on behalf of language, meaning, and truth. The words I write are not merely about themselves but are directed away from the page itself, straight up to you now as you read them. In other words, this is not so much a book about how words are used or what they mean, as it is about how words point beyond themselves to mean something between us as a writer and readers and, in general, to the meaning and reality and truth, whether mundane or ultimate, of what we think and say. This book is a thought-experiment on the relationship between Truth and truth, or Reality and our knowledge and experience of it.

Acknowledgments: Friends and colleagues Nick Barber, Martha Gill, Laura Long, Matt Pacetti, and Matthew Zilske, and Webb School of Knoxville students Grace Ding (Class of 2007), and Sam Bacon, John Haydek, Ryan Markman, and Carolyn Treasure (Class of 2008) proof-read and edited this manuscript to improve greatly the clarity, accuracy, and precision of its style and content. A special work of thanks goes to my good friend Ben Taylor, who spent an inordinate amount of time with me discussing and debating the foundational issues and theories of this book. Many thanks, finally, to Jim Tedrick of Wipf & Stock Publishers for his assistance in preparing this manuscript for publication. I have dispensed with most internal documentation for this non-scholarly book, but please see the Bibliography for a list of sources.

Todd_Speidell@webbschool.org

If you don't know where you're going, any road will take you there.

Φ George Harrison

A Narrative Beginning

It's weird starting life anew, Addy contemplated. Here I am, accepted and matriculated at Soteria University. I hadn't ever anticipated that I'd attend a university in Greece, but their mission statement struck me to my core: "Learn to be literate, erudite, and whole." Seemed quite grandiose to me—educating the whole person, mind, body, and soul!—but, hey, going to college abroad, who could complain? Plus, wholeness for me meant leaving behind, I hoped with all of my being, problems I thought should not be part and parcel of childhood.

I feel like the protagonist, Binx, in Walker Percy's (1916-1990) novel *The Moviegoer*. I'm reading this book at a time in my life when I can relate to a search for meaning in my life.

> The search is what anyone would undertake if he were not sunk in the everydayness of his own life. This morning, for example, I felt as if I had come to find myself on a strange island. And what does such a castaway do? Why, he pokes around the neighborhood and he doesn't miss a trick. To become aware of the possibility of the search is to be onto something. Not to be onto something is to be in despair. The movies are onto the search, but they screw it up: the search always ends in despair. They like to show a fellow coming to himself in a strange place—but what does he do? He takes up with the local librarian, sets about proving to the local children what a nice fellow he is, and settles down with a vengeance. In two weeks' time he is so sunk in everydayness that he might just as well be dead.

I've been dead for as long as I can remember, even though I hadn't realized during each moment of chronological time my gradual process of decay. The summer between my eighth grade and freshman year of high school highlighted a transition to a nice new town, a big new house, and the possibility of the excitement of fitting into circles of friends at an elite prep school, while leaving behind, albeit somewhat sadly my acquaintances, the sorrows of growing up in an environment of *everydayness*: life as mundane, full of routine but not of passion, like Mom and Dad's lives and relationship. They had benignly ignored each other, essentially living separate lives, presumably to tolerate each other for my sake. Dad sporadically marched through the house, shouting to all of us, "Seize the day!," but what he *really* meant was enigmatic to all of us and certainly most ambiguous to me. And if his message was truly important, why wasn't he here to deliver it more personally and constantly to his loved ones?

And then I found friends for the first time in my life, especially in the gatherings after the football games: companions who accepted me and apparently and purportedly loved me, despite my hang-ups and quirks and uncertainties. I felt loved.

Then, for the first time, I felt something—anything perhaps, but it seemed like something real—that I hadn't experienced even in my own family. It seemed like the first relationships I had felt, so long as nothing interfered with our *real* reasons for being together.

But then came the gods, and oh, how they meddle, with their letters home about how I was not quite living up to parental expectations for scholastic success. My need for a deeper intervention—even unwanted interference would have been finally welcomed!—was perceived only by my most wise and intuitive teachers, but they were reluctant to broach a delicate matter with a new family of pedigreed credentials.

My parents, however difficult it was for them, forgave me for needing to continue and complete my high school education in rehab. The parties, the notes home from teachers, and the conferences focused on my not living up to my "potential," and even a couple of friends, who were more aware and courageous than I led them to speak up on my behalf, even though my parents could not hear what I tried oh so desperately to say—all of these voices added up to one message: Addy needed help.

Maybe that's why I'm here, chasing after all this college knowledge, too. So when they asked us in Freshman Orientation to keep a journal during the course, and to kick it off with a little what-have-you about why I'm here and what I hope to gain from the whole experience, I decided to go ahead and just be as honest as hell. And I know hell—if anything, it's honest, and painfully so. So to be honest, I'm going to college not to get ahead in the world, because I was already born well beyond the starting line due to my promising and expecting origins. And please forgive me if I indulge in an excessive paralysis of analysis. It is quite annoying, I know. Yet perhaps later you might thank me, for I have the sneaking suspicion that depression signaled the only sign of genuine sanity I ever knew. Weird, huh? Were it not for the steady flow of alcohol and other drugs, provided by friends and sometimes by their parents, too, I might have realized earlier that I was in psychic pain.

Now on the eve before my first college class, I've arrived at the door of my G.A. to check on announced required readings before the first class. His name is Shema, and he announces on his door the following message:

> Pay no attention to those who teach that because Pythagoras listened to music, we now have the greater gift of mathematics. They know neither of music, nor of mathematics. What they call "sound wisdom" is merely foolish dissonance unworthy of being heard. For they themselves are not capable of *listening*.
>
> Φ From the *Scribblings* of Sonorous Maximus

When I knocked on the door, and a man who appeared close to my parents' age but seemed somehow more empathic and sagacious, opens the door and turns down a blaring but soulful Susan Tedeschi, I thought or rather intuited, this moment is analogous to something, to what, I couldn't say, but in some way I knew that I was onto something new.

"Fear and trembling before the gods?" Shema asked with a playful but endearing amusement. And I knew, with no explanation or comprehension, that I was indeed onto something.

It is my view that the weakening of authentic philosophy in our century has resulted in a form of collective and individual pathology that has far deadlier consequences than is generally imagined. We live in a time of metaphysical repression and this repression must be lifted. The various forms of psychological and sexual repression that modern psychiatry has successfully fought against are nothing when compared to the stifling of the love of meaning, which phrase actually is the definition of philosophy. The love of meaning, the search for meaning, is the only real, objective force for good in the life of modern man. Everything else we hope for and wish for ourselves and our children depends upon it.

Φ Jacob Needleman

Thought and language are not attempts to get in touch with reality, but attempts to find more imaginative ways of describing reality.

Φ Richard Rorty

"Introduction to Cultural Studies and Diversity"

While Addy sat in anxious anticipation inside a large lecture hall, looking around at the mass of strangers that constituted her fellow freshmen, Shema entered the lecture hall and announced, "Good morning, students. I'm the Graduate Assistant for this course, as many of you already knew. I'll be giving lectures, meeting with you in tutorials, reading and grading your papers, and helping and provoking you to make this course an eye-opening, and maybe even ear-opening, one for you in your freshman year at Soteria University. Our first week of classes will consist of the following schedule:

Monday: A dialogue today between Professors Univocal and Equivocal. As you knew from Freshman Orientation, you should have by now purchased the reader for this course and read the selected readings by Mortimore Adler and Jacques Derrida. Also, at your earliest convenience, read the materials by Adler on how to read intelligently and deeply, on how to speak and, just as importantly, on how to *listen* during intelligent conversation. [Note to reader: see the Appendix to this book.]

Wednesday: A dialogue between Professors Cacophonous and Harmonious. Please read the Jean-François Lyotard and Thomas F. Torrance selections prior to class.

Friday: I will lecture, or indulge in Socratic musings, which will be followed by an optional tutorial for those of you who desire further mind-stretching for your first week of university life, and please read the Søren Kierkegaard essay in preparation for that experience."

Addy liked the way that Shema emphasized *listen*, even though she wasn't quite sure why he seemed to prioritize its importance, but she had come a long way to listen, and her first class was about to begin. Shema continued by introducing the first lecturers, Profs. Univocal and Equivocal, who were ready to pontificate.

Prof. Univocal: Students, I must confess straight away that I am bothered. The relatively recent turn in philosophy from the quest for objective truth and meaning in life to constructing one's personal meaning is pure mind control, linguistic censorship, and metaphysical repression!

Prof. Equivocal: I think I know what you mean, Prof. Univocal, and you've piqued my curiosity, so please continue.

Univocal: It's just that for centuries philosophical thinking was preoccupied with the big questions: Who am I? What is my purpose in life? What is *yours*? What is *ours*? How can I live a truly fulfilling life? Socrates sought with an earnest heart the answers to these questions. He believed deeply in truth, as well as in both the individual and collective responsibilities needed to attain clarity in such matters. Mired in the skeptical relativism of our age, we seem largely apathetic to these quite grand yet seemingly basic questions. I believe this apathy is due to a loss of what

I call *common-sense* realism, which comprises these key points:

1. We have a common and universal human mind despite all our cultural diversity.
2. A reality exists that is independent of our minds.
3. Our minds can know and understand this objective reality.
4. We can talk intelligibly about reality to one another.

Equivocal: So you're saying we can all speak the same language?

Univocal: In a loose sense, I am. Whenever my mechanic tries to explain my car troubles to me, or whenever I hear two computer aficionados jabbering on about some new program or another, I want to interject with, "In plain English, please!" And so whenever they stop and explain things in terms I understand, I often reply, "Now we're speaking the same language here!"

Equivocal: So you're saying that we human beings, regardless of age, culture, or language differences, are similar enough to explain our experiences in terms others will understand.

Univocal: Well, yes, and if we consider the classical world and its understanding of metaphysics, then I think you'll understand my reasons for believing why this is so, and why I believe the critics of metaphysics have done more harm than good to the modern human mind.

Equivocal: Interesting, but please elaborate on your view on this paradigm shift in metaphysics.

Univocal: Traditional metaphysics assumes that the world of our everyday reality is as we generally experience it. It assumes that there are, in fact, cats, dogs, birds, men, women, children, the rain, and the moon, and everything else in-between. It assumes you see the green grass, too. You and I can both agree that a cat is a cat, that we feel the rain when it is raining, and that we enjoy the moon when it is full.

Traditional metaphysics, which literally means "after" or "above" physics, seeks to ask key questions about the nature of reality. I believe that philosophy went awry when it began to question mundane common sense, to deny the ultimate *reality* behind the patterns and laws governing the everyday natural world that we experience and understand. Rather than questioning the reality and knowledge of our everyday experience, traditional metaphysics seeks to take a step back and look at life from a larger scale or perspective.

Equivocal: To get the big picture, so to speak.

Univocal: Exactly. Are there greater forces or more fundamental principles behind the laws of nature? Can we distinguish general patterns in nature and human behavior and then construct a model locating our position and role in the cosmos, thereby deriving any meaning or purpose of our existence? Such are the questions metaphysics seeks to answer, and epistemology, properly so, is the attempt to *justify* our answers.

Equivocal: In other words, is there really a God, and what does it truly mean to be human? And to answer these questions, we can "read" nature (both human and non-human), much like a text, understanding its movements and discovering what it says to us, about us, and how we should respond to it.

Univocal: Yes, it is very much like a language. Just as we put vocabulary into syntax to form sentences and sentences together to form paragraphs and paragraphs together to form entire volumes of books, so in nature we also find a language of meaning. Through metaphysics we can learn this language, get *in touch with* reality, and find meaning and purpose for our lives.

Equivocal: And you believe we've deviated in some way, that we've stopped listening somehow?

Univocal: Yes. In fact, whether we realize it or not, some contemporary philosophies, such as postmodernism and poststructuralism, have abandoned even the possibility to understand the language of objective reality beyond the perspectives of different individuals. In doing so, we have lost touch with the syntax and semantics of reality itself! Most traditional philosophies were characterized by a greater emphasis on objective truths, meanings, and methods whose validity was independent of human experience. Though human experience was vital, the reality of independent truth was never questioned. This reality provided the basic starting point for the practice of much traditional philosophy, and common-sense experience of being in touch with reality and discussing it with clear and common public discourse is a given in one's search for truth and meaning in life.

Equivocal: I think I caught a glimpse of a pun in your use of the word "touch."

Univocal: Yes, a connotation of "syntax"—syn*tactic, tactile, touchable.* Isn't it interesting that the words *text, texture,* and even *textile* share the same root? It is as though through writing we can touch our words and feel the meanings we intend. And just as we might weave together threads of meaning, so we might also follow such threads in nature and uncover the emergence of an even greater pattern of which we are a small part.

Equivocal: I prefer the associations with *syn*thetic and *tac*tical. Could it not be that we are the ones who synthesize our own patterns out of randomness and nothingness, and through our *tac*tics and *tech*niques of power, impose these meanings upon others, thus creating our own realities?

Univocal: We will attend to that soon enough. For now, let's just say that metaphysics as traditionally practiced moves more along the lines of my own little word play.

Equivocal: I'll behave. Seriously, though, would you say that now with the new physics, quantum mechanics, etc., we don't have such a solid model to go by as we used to?

Univocal: Not at all, and I'll get to that soon enough. However, I do believe modern physics is a result of philosophical trends that are more troublesome. These trends have their roots in 19th century philosophy and science and have been an important cause of the violence, depravity, and utter absurdity of life many in the west have experienced this past century.

Equivocal: Elaborate on that concept a bit . . .

Univocal: Well, to understand this charge, I believe we need to back-peddle a bit to the French philosopher, mathematician, and scientist Descartes (1596-1650). I believe we both can agree that the central concern in modern philosophy, from Descartes onward, has been the problem of individual knowledge: "How can *I* know what is true?"

Equivocal: Precisely. Descartes theorized a model of the universe separated into two distinct realms: mind and matter. The human mind is separate from the material world and therefore cannot experience it directly. Only through certain innate ideas and logical deduction can we know anything of the world of matter with any certainty.

Univocal: Yes, and the Scottish philosopher David Hume (1711-1776) was an agnostic skeptic who played an important role in demonstrating the shaky foundation of this Cartesian argument. Hume could not be certain of the existence of God. If the mind knows only its states, then its states are all that it can know. If we can only experience the various states of our own minds and have no verifiable proof of the existence of other minds or objects, then our belief in them is irrational.

Equivocal: In other words, though we may see images flash across a TV screen, we have no idea of what is going on at the broadcasting end of the signal nor can we be certain that our receiving equipment functions correctly.

Univocal: Precisely.

Equivocal: And this is where Kant enters the picture.

Univocal: Indeed. The German critical philosopher Kant (1724-1804) felt compelled to counter Hume's skepticism. Kant agreed that we experience the empirical world only through the internal mechanisms of our subjective minds. These cognitive mechanisms organize our sense experiences into coherent interpretations of our perceptions, so that we can formulate conceptions of our experiences. By knowing the possibilities and the limits of how our minds function, what they are capable of knowing and not knowing, we can rest assured that we will not be led astray by irrational thinking.

Equivocal: So Kant takes Descartes' theory a step farther, developing his notions of innate ideas into synthesizing structures within the mind. Because our senses are continuously and often simultaneously bombarded by stimuli, our minds need to synthesize these stimuli into orderly, rational pictures and explanations. The catch is that we cannot know what these objects are really like in themselves but only as they appear to us based on how our minds construct them.

Univocal: And here lies the heart of our problem. If we can only know objects as they appear to us, then we cannot know them as they really are. This is where modern philosophy branched off yet again into contending factions. On the one hand, positivists maintained that empirically observable phenomena are the only things we experience, hence advocating science without metaphysics. They denied the possibility of knowing things in themselves simply because we had no direct experience of them. If something cannot be experienced, we should conclude that it does not exist . . .

Equivocal: On the other hand, constructivists concerned themselves with how the human mind and its ideas shape our views and understandings of our world. For constructivists, in general, we cannot get past our own personally and culturally constructed views to experience any kind of so-called objective reality.

Univocal: A bit of deadlock . . .

Equivocal: Sounds as if traditional metaphysics hit a slump, much like the Red Sox for nearly a cursed century! I can see what you mean by metaphysical repression.

Univocal: It gets worse. In the first half of the twentieth century, a series of scholars responded to both of these trends by attempting to show that there was indeed an underlying structure in human life. They were inspired by Ferdinand de Saussure (1857–1913), the Swiss founder of modern linguistics. Saussure sought to show that human language possessed a natural structure that determined relationships between the words we use and the meanings that we associate with them. The scholars inspired by Saussure, or structuralists, as they came to be called, believed this structure to be fixed and stable. Human beings in their everyday lives were not aware of it and so could not consciously change it. This structure, more than their conceptions, determined their behavior and ways of life.

Equivocal: And then along came the famous, or perhaps you'd prefer infamous, *poststructuralists*!

Univocal: In the early 1960s, a group of scholars challenged structuralists by demonstrating that this underlying structure is neither fixed nor stable. It is not a part of nature and certainly not innate to human nature. It is, rather, a result of the relationships of power in societies. That is, the many ways in which human beings influence one another, from everyday interactions at home, work, or school, all the way to the elite corridors of academic, social, political, and economic institutions, determine the shape of human social life. This shape was constantly changing, had no ultimate goal or meaning to it, and was the result of random collisions of power among human beings.

Equivocal: Just as certain scientists believed that the natural world was just a myriad of random collisions and interactions, they believed human social life was similarly conceived.

Univocal: As such, human life had no meaning, direction, or ultimate moral purpose upon which it could anchor itself. There was no right or wrong, no grand political design or ethical system that could be claimed to be best or even better than any other.

Equivocal: So how does all this relate to the changes in 20th century science?

Univocal: Well, I believe that those changes were heavily influenced by these philosophical trends.

Equivocal: How so?

Univocal: Well, quantum theory in physics is a primary example. It states that we cannot measure with absolute certainty the attributes of subatomic particles. This is the definition of Heisenberg's (1901-1976) uncertainty principle. Any attempt to measure them fundamentally alters them. We try to measure an electron's exact position, but then we lose the possibility of measuring its momentum or even its spin. Furthermore, the behavior of these particles, according to this theory, seems to be governed by random probabilities. We cannot predict with accuracy where electrons are going to be, where they are coming from, or what their particular characteristics are at any given moment.

Equivocal: So what has been the consensus in the scientific community?

Univocal: Well, herein lies the absurdity. They concluded that these particles do not possess any characteristics until they are actually measured. We endow them with their characteristics whenever we try to measure them. In other words, we take from reality what we want to see, rather than actually observing what is there and allowing that to mold our conclusions.

Equivocal: Could there not be hidden elements or variables that we have not yet discovered? Or perhaps could we not wait for more advanced technology to help us measure more clearly and accurately?

Univocal: "No!" was the absolute and resounding answer (and this was in the

1920s, mind you!). According to Niels Bohr (1885-1962) and the leading scientists of the established, orthodox quantum theory, modern science and technology can't arrive at a greater technology or devise a more intelligent experiment to determine the true nature of atoms and their constituent parts. The basic nature of reality is unknowable, and that's that. Go home and stop asking questions, thank you!

Equivocal: I could see how the implications could be troublesome, especially for the practice of metaphysics.

Univocal: Well, quantum theorists state that the very basic building blocks of our universe, of reality in general, are at their very best clouded, if not determined, by our mere subjective views of them, and do not possess a reality of their own. According to the scientists, we are standing on a groundless ground of nothingness, and that explains the true nature of all things!

Equivocal: So to summarize the philosophical and scientific trends of the past two centuries, at least as you perceive them:

> 1. We no longer possess a model of reality to describe our universe.
> 2. Therefore, we can understand neither our true nature as human beings nor the true nature of the world around us.
> 3. As a result, we cannot rely upon the traditional ethical systems to guide us in our relationships with other human beings. No one person, group of people, or institution has the authority to determine which system is better or best. In fact, if you are powerful enough, you can do whatever you want. What is right or wrong anyway? Who are we to judge the actions of other humans when their views are just as valid as our own?

Univocal: This is exactly what I mean by metaphysical repression. The methods of thought and conversation that enabled us at one time to access the reality of the universe, a reality that is capable of showing us the way things are, how they operate, how we might operate within them, and how we might construct a model to understand it all, have been discredited, shut down, and considered taboo by the intellectual establishment. Even the mere possibility is cut off by that one irritating question: Who's to say what's true or false?

Equivocal: If I believe it is true, then it's true for me.

Univocal: Exactly. But I have ranted far too long. I have not allowed you your chance to elaborate on your interpretation of metaphysical repression, which most certainly differs extensively with my own.

Equivocal: I love the statement "metaphysical repression," much as I do "thought control" and "linguistic censorship." I believe, however, that metaphysical repression means the repression coming from metaphysics. I believe it is metaphysics itself that is repressive. I also believe that the dualist epistemology that you claim ruined metaphysics has actually been a basic starting assumption of the traditional western philosophical tradition.

Univocal: Now that's interesting. Do continue, please.

Equivocal: I believe it goes back to the ancient Athenian philosopher Plato (428-347 BC), the founding father of the tradition. He was deeply concerned with the way things appear to us and the way they really are and how we might know the difference between the two. For him, our everyday world that we see, experience, and feel, was not the real world. The real world was the ideal world of the forms. For Plato, this world could be accessed through a quasi-mystical journey into the mind. Nevertheless, this basic dual distinction between the ways we commonly experience the world and the way it really is has been a deeply ingrained assumption that western philosophy has never been able to shake completely, though there have been serious attempts to do so.

Univocal: I find this dualist metaphysics problematic as well, but at least Plato does not question the independent nature of truth. Even though Plato believed we could access truth by searching our minds, he still believed in truth that was not dependent upon our own individually subjective experience.

Equivocal: I find this absolute idea of truth to be absurd. We are in a moment of transition today from a way of thinking that is determined for us by the authority of institutionalized power to ways of thinking determined for us by aspirations determined by the needs of individuals, communities, and cultures. We are experiencing the growing pains of greater maturity in which we can trust ourselves to determine what we need and what we want to accomplish with our lives.

Univocal: And without some form of a reality check, without some objective standard, don't you think we might lose ourselves?

Equivocal: I contend that we have been lost from the very beginning because we have relied on someone else's assumptions and methods of knowledge about the nature of reality. We feel lost today because we still have not yet realized fully that there is, in fact, nothing wrong with us and that all will not fall to pieces if we simply let go of our preconceived notions of true and false, right and wrong, good and evil, and trust our own instincts and intuitions. In fact, all that has been "wrong" up until now has been the result of the collective delusion that there is something wrong!

Univocal: And what does language have to do with these binary oppositions, these violent hierarchies, as you call them? Recall Plato's pupil Aristotle's (384-322 BC) theory of language: We use spoken words as symbols to represent—re-*present*—experience of reality, and we use written words to represent spoken words. How can we know that words, be they spoken or written, are accurate representations of our thoughts about reality?

Equivocal: My answer is that we cannot trust sense perception as a foundation for knowledge, as if there were an easy correspondence between the world out there and our understanding of it. However, traditional metaphysics attempts to answer this epistemological gap by appealing to something that transcends our everyday sense experience and yet is present inside us all along, whether one names it god, logos, truth, or nature. Ultimate reality, whatever one calls it, is supposed to be accessible by the mind, and we simply need to think and speak about it in just the right way so that we will get it right and so will everyone else.

Univocal: Hence, *meta*-physics: a reality beyond physical reality! It is something that transcends this physical reality, and it is imperative that we understand it on its own terms!

Equivocal: That kind of epistemological imperialism is also what makes metaphysics repressive! What happens when you cannot access reality "on its own terms"? What happens when what appears self-evident to others doesn't appear self-evident to you? There are perhaps two distinct possibilities in this case:

1. You don't have it and there's something wrong with you, so you better get it! OR:
2. You don't have it because it's not there, and there is nothing wrong with you!

So I would say, to conclude, that language and thought cannot be attempts to get in touch with reality because we've never been disconnected from reality to begin with, as we have come to think. So instead of asking the great question, "What is the nature of reality?," why not ask, "What is it that compels me to even ask that question?"

A Narrative Interlude on Incredulity

Incredulous, a philosophy major and a fellow freshman, had eyed Addy during class as he considered that Prof. Equivocal was trouncing Prof. Univocal.

The pressures and adventures of adult living, especially leaving behind a stable home, both emotionally and economically, and facing the prospects of a career in philosophy became increasingly prominent in his life, and yet he could not see himself preparing for life in a gray flannel suit. Though he had renounced faith in any essential meaning to life, he did not lose all hope for a life lacking in meaning either. For he believed that any meaning would have to be the meaning he himself chose for it. He certainly would not find it out there around a corner waiting on him. So he decided to pursue the ways of the philosophers, more to hear their questions than their answers even though he questioned both. Instead of simply accepting their formulations, he brought a refreshingly new way of thinking, even though rooted in the manner of the ancients, a radically disconcerting questioning of everything.

Incredulous was always fascinated by the question of belief. After the great revolutions, political as well as intellectual, when the philosophers rose to power over the priests and theologians, they replaced God with Man, and faith with reason. They called religion and tradition "irrational," and reason and science "rational." But what was so different between the two? Was not the second a type of "religious" persuasion too? With that question, he made many people angry, especially the congregants of the Church of Reason (as he liked to call it). Believing students in the philosophy department agreed with his critique of the religious fervor of Enlightenment reason, until he turned his relentless attack on faith toward the pious as essentially "fellow believers" or "kissing cousins" of Enlightenment intellectuals! Enlightenment faith in Man simply made Man into God, whereas pious believers made God out of Man!

Incredulous thought that while reason might be able to demonstrate validity through various forms of reasoning, it could not demonstrate why it should be privileged over all other forms of human experience, as if it were the only legitimate way to make choices and understand life. Why not intuition or emotion or tradition or faith or even coin-tossing? What makes reason so special? What makes any of them so special? If none of them can demonstrate its own validity, then none of them can claim supremacy over any other. Of course, different ways of experiencing life should be respected, but we do not have to be so uptight about "getting it right." Life, whatever it may be, will not allow us to do so. History is merely a continual succession of a multiplicity of worldviews and ways of life, sometimes fighting and overthrowing each other, sometimes merging peacefully together, or sometimes splintering into a thousand tiny pieces. And some viewpoints will grow to be great, and many others will slip away into the oblivion and silence of the past, perhaps never to be heard from again. Multiplicity is nothing to fear, really. If that's just the way it is, then how could it be otherwise? How could it be "right" or "wrong" or "good" or "bad"?

These questions and counter-questions circled around his head while he listened to the professorial debate and continued to notice Addy. But within himself, at times barely noticeable even to himself, was a lingering wanting of "something more" than the cynical bankruptcy of mere incredulity, on the one hand, and a residual and wistful but grandiose longing for the reconciliation of reason and religion, on the other. So Incredulous *seeks* while finding himself hanging out under the cover of the nightlife, in clubs, bars, basements, and dives of all sorts, as well as in the high-browed obscurity of avant-garde galleries, chasing the whisperings of a name no one speaks aloud and yet scribbling it down onto college-ruled notebook paper.

Addy sat for a few moments when this introductory dialogue concluded, considering an exchange of opposing viewpoints an intriguing way to begin a course. Prof. Univocal's view seemed to mirror common sense, but Prof. Equivocal's stance was more sophisticated and seemed somehow deeper and more in tune with her search for greater meaning in life, especially amidst the chaos of things that seemed more prominent than any underlying order. Life seemed more fleeting than fixed. While she briefly mused to herself, Incredulous walked by and smiled at her, simply saying, "Good stuff, huh? See you next time!"

Although the expert[s] . . . can indicate their clues and formulate their maxims, they know many more things than they can tell . . .

Φ Michael Polanyi

Addy arrived to the next class early, both excited to hear the next dialogue and wondering if Incredulous would say hello to her again. Perhaps he was just being friendly. She didn't see him yet, but Shema briskly walked into the lecture hall and abruptly announced that it was time to begin. Today's class would feature a dialogue between Prof. Harmonious and Prof. Cacophonous.

Prof. Harmonious: Students, I advocate that the universe, the whole of reality, is an interrelated unity. In a dimly analogous fashion, it is much like a great symphony orchestra run by a master conductor. Here we find a diversity of instruments and sounds, each existing in an interdependent relationship with the rest to produce a sublimely unsurpassable beauty of sonorous unity. To comprehend this, I argue here that we must ever strive to attain "hearing eyes and seeing ears," as musical theory would have us, and tune into the multi-faceted inner workings of this great harmony in ever-greater breadth and depth. As we take down such notation, we might share it with others, so that they too may come to tune in with us, and in so doing point out even greater subtleties to us as well. As the process deepens, so will our joyful appreciation of the diverse unity that is the complex reality in which we dwell.

Prof. Cacophonous: Despite the beauty of Dr. Harmonious' words, we might remind ourselves that music is something that we create to provide us with a sense of unity, safety, and security in an otherwise disjointed and chaotic universe. Our knowledge as human beings reflects such chaotic reality. All of our attempts to construct a unified theory of all reality have been in vain. How often have we tried to create a theory of nearly everything, and how many times have we almost succeeded, only to discover gaping holes that brought it crumbling to the ground?

How often have we witnessed one scientific or philosophical view rise to prominence, only to be superseded by another, and still yet another? Is there no end in sight of such incongruous sounds? If we are to use metaphors of sound for such a description of reality, we might say that the nature of reality is not consonance but dissonance.

Harmonious: Because you see fragmentation in reality, I would like to discuss how such fragmented views have come about. These disjointed views are products of disjointed thinking! Such disjointed thinking arises from what the dualistic and abstractive thought that has wreaked havoc upon the Western mind. Modern appropriations of the thought of Plato and Aristotle have led to such a crisis. From Plato we have inherited the dualist notion of "mind-over-matter." From Aristotle we have the tradition that knowledge comes to the mind through our senses. These themes combined during the Enlightenment to give us the confused and misguided epistemology that is crumbling around us today, unable to properly integrate the external, material world with the inner, mental world? Such a mind-matter divide led Kant to tell us that our minds have built-in mechanisms that construct such appearances from sense experience, so that all that we can know is how things appear to us but not how they are in themselves. This perspective led to a deep epistemological disjunction with reality, a disjunction that of course is a form of mental illness, or psychosis. For what is a psychotic illness but one in which the patient is out of touch with reality?

It is upon this foundation that modern science and philosophy have built their methodologies, but it is a foundation with no solidity, left open to critical attacks of all forms, so that there is little doubt about the reasons for our crisis of knowledge today.

Cacophonous: We are experiencing a crisis of knowledge today, no doubt, as a result of the crumbling of philosophy's traditional foundations on which to construct a system of knowledge. There are, in fact, no foundations upon which we might build a truly objective knowledge of all things. To demonstrate this theory, we might look to history, at the transition between the Middle Ages and the Enlightenment. In the Middle Ages the final word on everything was the Word of God. A dramatic re-enactment of a pre-Enlightenment dialogue might proceed as follows:

"Why is such-and-such so?"

"Because the priest says so."

"How does the priest know?"

"He knows because the church knows, and it knows because it speaks for God, and if God said it, we believe it, and that's that."

"Oh, I see. Thanks."

This approach worked for awhile, but along came the Renaissance and the Protestant Reformation, and finally the Enlightenment, along with ever-increasing bold replies to the church: "Oh, I see. Thanks for your input, really. Yet it means absolutely nothing to me, and it is as irrelevant as are you."

In the modern era, such responses were replaced with a new sort of language game: "Science says so, as do the philosophers in the university who define what science can say. So I guess they're right . . . but who understands them anyway?"

The Enlightenment replaced the authority of God with the equally absurd authority of Man. Man could know anything he wanted to know, without worrying about what some god might think because, of course, Man was a god of sorts. Besides, the new "priests" of the order—the scientists and university professors—could explain it all to anyone who cared and, of course, had the time.

Yet who was this Man of whom so many were speaking? I've seen a lot of people but never a collective Man. The Enlightenment defined Man as the generic reasoning individual person, referred to in philosophical works as "the subject." When we speak of subjectivity, we refer to the philosophical reasoning and experience of the individual human being. Yet there were a lot of little subjects, and, of course, it was difficult getting them to agree. The state was not going to let all of us become arrogant little gods, each trying to shout down the rest. So the state replaced the church with a new one of even grander pretensions: the university. It, in compliance with state subsidies, including lifetime job security and pension schemes for the new professor-priests, became the arena to decide who was Man. We still have not finally decided who Man is or will finally be. As in professional boxing, this language game allows no one to hold the title for long. Yet if nobody can, why should we try? Why should anyone try so hard to "get it right," or attain the final, objective, and true theory that applies to anyone, anywhere, and at any time? Why is it that we feel it so necessary?

Harmonious: I agree with you in many ways. We inevitably fall short when we strive for divine, autonomous knowledge—as the first human couple attempted!—but we must not despair and should apply ourselves, open ourselves up, as it were, to real knowledge. It is not a dualistic matter of absolute Truth or no truth at all. Nor is it properly a question of whether or not my philosophy is better than or as good as yours, simply because each "works" fine for each of us. It is, rather, that our various philosophies, methodologies, and modes of rationality should properly hold up the knowledge of the truths we possess in the light of the intelligible universe—reality itself—and allow that to determine for us the validity of our own claims. Each of the truths we've discovered will and should be inevitably altered or modified in the light of reality. If we do not allow truth to radically challenge, even to shake the very foundations of our beings and minds, along with the terrible obliteration of lifestyles and ways of thinking we've constructed around us and once found to be certain, then we risk a most unfortunate doom—the hellish darkness of insanity, the nightmare of psychosis! For will we not have lost touch with reality?

Cacophonous: I am all in favor of continuous disruption of established truths. I would even be glad to engage in comparative contrasts of such truths in the light of truth, if such truth existed. Yet such a grand vision is merely a pipe dream. We cannot know or understand anything beyond our concepts, our little truths, and these are socially and culturally constructed. For would we not end up merely talking about our own ideas about things, lacking not only a basis for comparison but a common language of translation as well? To offer you an example, might I ask if you have you ever seen the film *The Gods Must Be Crazy*?

Harmonious: My word, no, but from the way you speak, I'm sure you have.

Cacophonous: Funny. However, the film begins with a glass Coca Cola bottle thrown from a prop-plane flying over the Kalahari Desert. It happens to land next to an indigenous member of the Khoi-San, or Bushman, as the movie refers to him, passing by. He has never seen such a strange object, but since he heard it fall and hit the ground, he knows that it came from the sky and therefore from the gods.

Harmonious: This does sound like madness, but continue please.

Cacophonous: Well, he infers the following: the bottle is a gift, a curse, or an object that someone dropped by accident. Nevertheless, he picks it up and takes it with him back to his home. He figures that if someone just dropped it and needed it back, then he would hold onto it for a few days and be prepared to gladly return it.

Harmonious: He sounds like an honorable and sensible fellow.

Cacophonous: Yes, a real stand-up guy. If it is a gift, then he will certainly show his gratitude. If it happens to be a curse, then he will make the necessary amends, and all will be well again. So he takes the "thing" back home, where it is happened upon by his family, who begin making merry use of it. It has several fascinating qualities, allowing it to perform many useful functions. Because it is hollow and solid, it could serve as a handy container for water. Yet it is also as hard as rock, making it useful for household maintenance and cooking tasks. Yet it also has a practical aesthetic appeal. It is clear and smooth, like water, and quite beautiful, providing decoration for the home. It also could be used to make pretty designs by dipping it at various points in dye and then applying it to clothing design and decorative apparel. It also makes a noise when someone blows air across the surface of its hole, and so it could be used to make music, which is always good. The family concludes that it must be a gift from the gods and so thanked them considerably for being so benevolent.

Harmonious: Gratitude is indeed an appropriate response to the reality of God's grace, and yet I sense that there is a down side to this crazy bottle.

Cacophonous: Indeed, for each person desires to use it all the time. Since there is only one bottle, they begin jealously fighting over it. Upon seeing this conflict, our hero knows now that it must be a curse from the gods, for only curses would cause such mayhem.

Harmonious: Sounds like the kind of confusion that has existed since the Tower of Babel! But please continue with this intriguing saga.

Cacophonous: So he tries to throw it back up to the gods, but it only falls down and hits one of his children. He then tries to bury it in the desert, but a hyena digs it up and brings it back. He then sets out on a journey to throw the evil thing off the edge of the world. Our story follows our protagonist as he searches for the edge of the world, or at least someone else whom, being more knowledgeable of this thing, might know what to do with this dreaded object.

Harmonious: What a delightful story. I must see it soon.

Cacophonous: It is one of my favorites. So what was this strange "thing?" To the Khoi-San, who had never seen something like this before, it was initially one thing, but then it was another and then another. It was many different things depending on its use or on someone's evaluation of it. Though you might be tempted to say, "We know it was just a Coca-Cola bottle. The

Khoi-San, however, didn't have that information, and had we had a chance to lead them out of the Kalahari into the nearest bottling factory of then Botswana, they would have understood well that it was not worth the fuss." Yet was it just that? Was it not also transformed into something else through incorporation within the linguistic and cultural universe of the Khoi-San?

Harmonious: I can also see that if we follow the life of the bottle," we might see that it was many different things at different times even to us: marketed product, shapeless glass, empty bottle, sealed bottle, desired solution to hunger and thirst, useless trash to be thrown out the window of a low-flying prop-plane. Yes, I can see your point.

Cacophonous: Yes, and let us not forget what it might become through our recycling technologies. My point is that to take something so simple as an everyday soda bottle and to define it once and for all is really just arbitrary. It depends on where and when you stand to make that call.

Harmonious: Yes, from that way of thinking I can understand how you might arrive at that conclusion. Yet that is only one way of understanding the phenomenon at hand. It is also a very narrow way of thinking. I call it a "techno-logical" way of thinking. It begins with us, with our experiences, with our estimates and use-values of the phenomena we encounter, and then proceeds to define other phenomena in those terms alone. What our protagonist does is a sort of mini-account of what we have done for quite some time in our own culture with our scientific inquiries into the nature of the universe. Notice that upon encountering the bottle in the desert, he immediately concludes that it must be from the gods, which, of course, within his particular cosmology, would be a reasonable conclusion. Yet he initially proceeds wisely in forgoing a hasty conclusion and suspends the question for a few days pending further information from reality outside of his own perception. Meanwhile, someone stumbles across it and starts experimenting with it, thereby starting the whole chain of events and their results, both beneficial and harmful. Yet we see the process by which the bottle itself becomes trapped within the Khoi-San cultural and linguistic system of signs and symbols, and how they begin to define what the bottle "is" by what it does for them and to them. So the bottle becomes simply what they make of it. So it is good or evil, a gift or a curse, depending on how they view it.

So at first our friend, and I mean no disrespect towards him, behaved as a good scientist. He encountered a strange and unknown phenomenon, instinctively conjectured some likely possibilities based on *a priori* assumptions but reasonably set these aside, allowing himself time to ponder and await further information. Nevertheless, he ended as a bad technician, allowing prior experience to determine the nature of the unknown. He then discarded this unknown phenomenon before ever knowing it.

Cacophonous: Aren't you being a bit unfair to our hero? How could he know what a scientist or technician, either good or bad, would do in such situations? Furthermore, how would he know how to proceed, if he had no concept of existence beyond his immediate world of the Kalahari?

Harmonious: Well, how is anything new ever discovered? Take Einstein (1879-1955), for example. He made several significant discoveries for which no one had the slightest concept, or even the technology for their verification until years after. He did so with neither a Ph.D. degree nor the backing of the major governmental and scientific institutions in Europe at the time.

Cacophonous: Yes, but Einstein at least had historical precedence and scientific methodology available to provide a minimal backdoor into the formulation of such theories. What are we to make of the Khoi-San? How could they have even known how to proceed from there to truly inquire into the nature of this object? All they had to go on was the tenuous presence or absence of the gods. Had our hero waited on the gods, he would have never known anything about this strange object.

Harmonious: And yet he did not wait upon the gods, did he? He set out to find the end of the earth so as to dispose of it.

Cacophonous: True enough, but seeking neither guarantees success nor indicates that he was proceeding in any way we might call "scientific." He was by no means "objective" and had already established his conclusion firmly in his mind. He was not setting out to discover the true nature of this object but to find a way to rid himself of it. So to say he was or was not behaving scientifically or objectively imposes upon him a cultural concept that did not exist in his mind.

Harmonious: Perhaps it is a fundamental epistemic concept that a lot of philosophers of today need to have imposed upon their minds! You cannot know the universe in all its multifaceted splendor based on the comfort of the familiar, which would be a profound misunderstanding of scientific discovery. Thankfully, great minds like Einstein and the British biochemist and philosopher Michael Polanyi (1891–1976) have taught us an important lesson in this regard, given the priority of the reality of the object under investigation to unfold and impose itself upon our inquiring but incomplete minds. It is a dualistic assumption that reality can't be known, with the unfortunate consequence that one may impose one's own perspective, whatever it happens to be, upon reality. Perhaps we could see that it was under the impulse of the utterly strange otherness of this object that our hero sets out from the familiarity of his home to seek out the "edge of the world," the frontier between the known and the great unknown beyond, that was truly objective, truly scientific. Perhaps, our friend was behaving far more scientifically than many "self-proclaimed" scientists today. Perhaps we should integrate this film as required viewing into curricula across the globe. Many of our future scientists could benefit from such bold metaphors.

Cacophonous: Now I would definitely love to show this film in my classes. However, there is another question of significance I wish to pose. It is the question of "objectivity." Can we ever move beyond our socially and culturally constructed concepts of the world? If we can only speak using concepts of what we already know, how can we know anything new? Would it be anything really new, or simply a rearranging of our old concepts into a slightly novel formation? How is it that we can describe anything apart from concepts, for are we not simply using more concepts?

Harmonious: To answer these questions, there are two important components, or coefficients, as I call them, of all knowledge—the subjective and the social coefficients. The subjective coefficient deals with personal experience, and the social coefficient with collective experience. Neither of these can be avoided unless somehow we could live in a vacuum. However, both require reality to maintain a certain degree of independence from our manipulation of it. *Reality speaking to us* is a methodological priority that takes precedence over converting the widely acknowledged subjective and social coefficients of knowledge into a methodological axiom that would preclude personal and collective participation in and knowledge of objective reality. We need to learn to listen as reality speaks.

Relationships with human beings function in a healthy manner when we as personal subjects learn to hear the other. We must first of all acknowledge the reality of the other's objective existence as truly other, not to be manipulated or shaped to fit our own preconceived ideas or expectations. The other has the proper role of dictating to us how he or she may be known. This basic principle of knowledge, that is, that reality speaks to us and we must learn to listen, is true on personal, social, collective, natural, and other levels of existence, even though of course we must adapt how we listen to each unique object or subject.

So while we communicate through languages and the cultural worldviews they express, the subjective and social coefficients of knowledge demonstrate a human capacity to be affected by modifications of our consciousness through encounters with what is independently real. We do not have to be confined by our biased concepts nor do we have to forever descend in the vicious cycle of prejudice—otherwise, progress on social, scientific, or other fronts would not be possible.

Cacophonous: I agree that people change their perspectives, but this in no way illustrates that one has achieved an inherently better or more accurate view. Circumstances are continuously changing, and new information produces altered viewpoints almost constantly. Yet I cannot ascertain that such changes inevitably lead to a more objective viewpoint than any other. Besides, have we not witnessed a great number of philosophical, religious, scientific, and even political changes of mind throughout history, some of which seem better, some seem worse, and some seem only to be what they are: just changes? Even words such as "better" or "worse" merely indicate value judgments of our own specific time and circumstances, for were not these changes viewed during their own moments better to some people and worse to others, depending on who was commenting? Are not all observations of what is true and false dependent upon value judgments that cannot ultimately be demonstrated, either empirically or rationally, to be valid for all people? And if people claim to speak objectively in the name of truth, do they not presuppose that their own values are superior to those of different voices? Do they ultimately and surreptitiously seek to silence these potentially oppositional perspectives?

Harmonious: I agree that this form of pseudo-objectivity, as you and others have previously defined it but what I would call objectivism, is an impossible and undesirable absurdity. To say that we can ignore our personal feelings, desires, passions, the socially and culturally constituted concepts of our languages, the immediate demands of our historical circumstances, and the needs of the communities in which we live, and finally step away from it all and supra-personally transcend to absolute and final knowledge, would be a statement of a lunatic. Such a goal lies at the heart of the positivism that infects modern philosophy. Yet a belief in true objectivity, or the universal intent of personal knowledge, does not commit one to objectivism, which deludes itself into believing that one can eliminate the person from knowledge.

Cacophonous: I agree with your last point, but how would your definition of objectivity avoid the naïve ideology of objectivism?

Harmonious: Remember that objectivity is not something I possess when I am investigating something—the pseudo-objectivity of so-called enlightened reason, which is the worst form of subjectivity and a key point on which you and I agree—but it is controlled by the very object of investigation. I must allow its uniqueness to speak to me, altering my understanding of it, rather than allowing my preconceived ideas of reality or arbitrary will to somehow determine what it is. Rather than presuming to be autonomous experts in our fields of knowledge, standing over them in authority, we must submit ourselves humbly, respectfully, and patiently to the objects of our investigations. A radically and rigorously scientific conception demands that we become listening students of whatever reality we wish to know. Only then can we dare to speak about truth and reality as we continue to listen for the uniquely new and different to emerge again from repeated investigations. Only in this manner, as we listen and continue to listen, allowing our own knowledge to be modified again and again, can we truly say with any confidence that we possess objective knowledge at all. We have only one choice to make in any form of scientific or rational knowledge: We must acknowledge that reality dictates to us how we may approach it, so that reality in all its forms, whether natural or supernatural, will show us the unique and appropriate ways to understand reality on its own terms, thus deepening our knowledge of it.

Cacophonous: Your sense of objectivity supports what I am saying. It is because we, as individuals, communities, cultures, and nations, object or resist, that we cannot finally propose a fully satisfactory knowledge of human beings and of the cosmos, for there is always resistance to such views. There is always disagreement, disjunction, and disruption of all sorts, if only in brief moments or in tiny, almost insignificant minorities. Nevertheless, suppose we have two competing investigators. How do we know who is a better "listener" than the other? How are we, the uninformed, to conclude that one position or viewpoint is more objective than any other? Furthermore, supposing that there is a supposed objective reality that speaks to us and informs of its nature, how are we to listen? How are we to know what it is saying, especially if it does not speak directly in human language?

Harmonious: I'd like to recall two anecdotes from Albert Einstein's childhood. As a small boy, he received a compass from his father for his birthday. The immediate orientation of the needle to the north fascinated Einstein and interestingly led him from one little discovery, from one "Aha!" to another for years to come. One such "Aha" occurred at the age of sixteen, when he first imagined what it might be like if he could fly along next to a beam of light, traveling at the same speed. This imaginary excursion into the majestic realm of the cosmic would later serve him in his formulation of his theories of relativity. Einstein had an unshakable faith in the capabilities of his free imagination, and his passionate love for all things scientific would continually nurture his almost playfully childlike excursions. It was this faith, imagination, and love that constituted his primary epistemological tools for the discoveries that changed modern science.

Einstein never ceased listening to his own intuitive insights and trusting in his creative imagination. In 1905, at the age of twenty-six, having been rejected by all the graduate school programs to which he had applied, he produced not one, not two, but three of the most significant scientific contributions of our time, any one of which would have made him a legend in the human sciences on par with Galileo, Copernicus, Newton, and Clerk Maxwell. Each of these papers would later radically re-design 20th century science. In them, he proved the real existence of atoms, the particle nature of light, the relativity of time, space, and motion, and the fact that matter was simply another form of energy (his famous $E=mc^2$). Based on these discoveries, he opened the door for the new fields of quantum mechanics, nuclear engineering, and later, through the expansion of the Special to the General Theory of Relativity, to the field of cosmology (which studies the birth, expansion, and future of the known universe).

How could one so young, inexperienced, and lacking in accepted academic credentials depict natural phenomena with such startling accuracy? The tacit dimension of knowledge comes into play here, where the human mind intuitively and intimately comes into contact with the intelligible universe. As we are parts of the non-human universe, existing in an interdependent relationship with it, we naturally have points of contact with it besides our physical dependence upon it for our survival. We are capable of recognizing patterns in our everyday lives, and we cannot simply explain how we do so—the complex tasks of driving cars, recognizing people's faces, remembering vast amounts of information stored in our brains, and most amazingly of all, our use of languages. We know more than we can tell about the simplest of daily tasks. In the same way, we are also capable of recognizing ever greater and newer patterns through our learning processes. These same processes enable us to intuitively apprehend patterns in nature of which we do not always have an immediate, familiar contact.

Cacophonous: Yet if we cannot verify this intuitive apprehension, then how can we know they exist? Furthermore, how are we to know whose apprehensions function better, or how they are even "supposed" to function?

Harmonious: We all have those gut feelings, hunches, and "Aha's!"—key insights that make the whole picture fall together in perfect clarity—do we not? How does one know when another loves him or her except by an intuitive leap?

Cacophonous: But you sound like a naïve realist, no different than a misguided faith based either on religion or on reason, despite all your harmonious descriptions of the cosmos and how all persons have a distinctly important part in the grand symphony, which in fact is your own subjective symphony, or someone else's you are peddling. Is it not?

Harmonious: You are not listening, Cacophonous, and given your methodological axiom of hearing all and any voices, it is no surprise that you are hard of hearing! I am not saying that you must believe as I do or that you must accept what I say because I say so. If we acknowledge the true sense of objectivity, then control of the other, whether human or natural, will no longer be an issue. For acknowledging objectivity is ultimately to remain silent and to listen and to allow reality to speak for itself. Reality speaking to us and informing us of what we should know about it and how we should approach it refrains us first and foremost from final judgments, which will never be ours to make anyway, so that when it is our turn to speak, we may speak as if we were an honored guest in the home of another—with humble yet genuine understanding.

The great Danish philosopher Soren Kierkegaard's (1813-1855) incarnational realism anticipates Einstein when he describes a faith based on a personal penetration and knowledge of the eternal entering into time that dictates to us that we too move with the movement of time. The subjective and inward truth moves with the object of knowledge based on a deeper penetration into the richness of God's revelation in space and time. This is very far from a facile and dualistic contrast between objectivism, which misses the inner logic of incarnation, God's entering into time in one man in a particular time and place not accessible by the universal canons of reason, and subjectivism, a leap of faith based on one's *a priori* experience. The universal reason of objectivism is only a different *a priori* than the personal experience of subjectivism. In emphasizing the importance of a deep personal relation to God, Kierkegaard recognizes the shortcomings of objectivism and subjectivism, both giving priority to an autonomous subject in the apprehension of objects.

Cacophonous: You have told me nothing new, and you have not convinced me that there is anything but dissonance in the so-called universe.

Harmonious: Cacophonous, I cannot make you listen to beauty. All I can say is that as it is with all things, we must acknowledge objective reality and listen, so that our perceptions come into increasing conformity to what is real. Try listening for the sonority and harmony behind and beyond the cacophony of divergent voices, which are disruptive and dissonant in modern life and thought, until you are ready and able to listen.

The heated dialogue ended with Prof. Cacophonous giving Prof. Harmonious the cold shoulder in an agitated exit. Addy considered that Prof. Harmonious spoke boldly and confidently, which both appealed to her and yet made her wonder if she could countenance such confidence. Prof. Cacophonous, at least, heard one more voice than he could tolerate! Matters were even more complicated than she had thought after the first lecture, and she wondered if somehow the chaos of her own life would amount to more than a cacophony of meaningless noise but perhaps, she hoped, just perhaps there might be some underlying and overarching harmony that makes sense of things. She sat alone for several minutes as she contemplated the wonder and grandeur of it all.

The Incredulity of the Human Heart

He knocked softly upon her dorm room door. No answer. Obviously, she could barely hear it. He banged loudly on the aluminum door and filled the entire hallway with the racket. "Why not announce to the Sorbonne that you're here?" he muttered. The door had been slightly ajar, and when he saw her, he apologetically explained that he hadn't planned on picking her up for class.

Turning around to make a quick exit, he heard, "That you, Incredulous?," which Addy exclaimed as she woke from her nap and saw his silhouette.

"Yes, ready for class?" They went together to hear the philosophical musings of the mysterious Shema to wrap up the first week of their intriguing course.

If God held all Truth in His right hand, and in His left hand the lifelong pursuit of it, he would choose the left hand.

Φ Kierkegaard on Lessing

Shema was different, no doubt. It was in the way he moved: casually and carelessly, yet with a tacitly unpredictable grace that always seemed to make final sense. He was a graduate assistant, not an accomplished professor, but he spoke in a way that suggested he was onto something—that there's really something more meaningful to life than her burdened past would attest—as when he first asked Addy with a wry and penetrating wisdom, "Fear and trembling before the gods?"

He approached the podium as one who had learned to listen and not one who hastened to speak. "What I am about to tell you is terrifying. If there are those among you who suffer from a heart condition, or if perhaps you might think that you are pregnant, you would do well to step out for the remainder of this lecture and listen instead to the sweet nothingness of ignorance. Back in my office only a moment ago, I was warned not to speak of any of this to you. 'They are too young,' a tenured professor told me. 'Too inexperienced in life to begin to grasp these notions.' And this harkened me to a quotation from Jesus of Nazareth: 'I thank you, Father, that you have hidden your righteousness from the wise and the educated, and revealed it to innocents, to the babes and the unlearned.' And this is how I see you—and I am not insulting you! In fact, I am giving you the highest compliment imaginable, which is to be among those privileged few who hold the distinct honor of having accomplished nothing of their own in this life, and so therefore cannot lay claim to the title of expert at anything other than of being good and wise people who know how to inquire. Stay that way. If you have an inquiring mind, do not advance any farther in your lives! You've already accomplished more than most distinguished scholars! In fact, it is a sad commentary upon the current condition of humanity that western society would have us believe otherwise—that somehow you are only beginning your lives, and that there are many things waiting for you to accomplish once the intelligentsia inform you of their words of wisdom. Is it possible that the so-called experts might have missed something that is quite basic? Our language is loaded with such phrases, especially as professorial types offer their seasoned critiques of introductory students. How many times have I heard the comment: 'He'll turn out ok, I think . . . I hope.' I'm reminded of the line from the movie when Serpico asked a lady friend, 'Why is it that all your friends are on the their way to becoming somebody else?'

"The greatest statements made in the 20th century in the philosophy of language were not made by professional philosophers but by far the most unlikely of candidates. Though their joint discoveries took place at the end of the 19th century, they lived most of their lives in the 20th and so we'll claim them for that era. First and foremost was a twenty-two-year old woman who was almost completely blind, and secondly, was a seven-year-old girl from Tuscumbia, Alabama, who was blind, deaf, and mute.

Their work together demonstrated greater insight into the mystery of language than any other attempts that have been made before or since. They are, respectively, Anne Sullivan and Helen Keller.

"Anne Sullivan, who was orphaned as a baby, spent the first ten years of her life in a poor house before attending the Perkins Institute for the Blind in Boston, MA. The Keller family hired her as a personal tutor for Helen, which was to be her first and only teaching assignment.

"At the age of nineteen months, Helen survived a rare life-threatening illness that left her blind and deaf, and subsequently mute. Though she had learned to make sounds before this age, and even managed to pronounce the word 'wa-wa' for 'water,' her illness cut off any further development of language, and Helen spent her next six years in continuous darkness and silence. Then one strange day in 1887, she experienced a most remarkable breakthrough. Sullivan took her to the water pump outside the Keller family home, and placed her right hand under the running water, and in her left she spelled in sign the word 'water.' After repeated attempts, it finally dawned on Helen that w-a-t-e-r was the name for water. In her words (quoted in Walker Percy's *The Message in the Bottle*),

> We walked down the path to the well-house of the honeysuckle with which it was covered. Someone was drawing water and my teacher placed my hand under the spout. As the cool stream gushed over one hand, she spelled the word *water*, first slowly then rapidly. I stood still, my whole attention fixed upon the motion of the fingers. Suddenly I felt a misty consciousness as of something forgotten—a thrill of returning thought; and somehow the mystery of language was revealed to me. I knew then that "w-a-t-e-r" meant the wonderful cool something that was flowing over my hand. That living word awakened my soul, gave it light, hope, joy, set it free! There were barriers still, it is true, but barriers that could in time be swept away.

> I left the well-house eager to learn. Everything had a name, and each name gave birth to a new thought. As we returned to the house every object which I touched seemed to quiver with life. That was because I saw everything with the strange, new sight that had come to me . . .

"Helen then insatiably absorbed the wide world around her. She not only learned to communicate through sign but also to read, write, and speak. She went on to high school, graduated from college, and learned to speak French and German (some French speakers claimed her French was even better than her English). She lived a more enriching life than many in possession of their sight and hearing. Her life was filled with traveling, lecturing, swimming, and horseback riding. She was a copious reader and a prolific writer.

"Her story is as strikingly remarkable as it is deeply moving. After Helen's breakthrough moment at the well pump, she met her mother and her father for the first time. In fact, she knew herself for the first time. At the age of ten she spoke her first sentence ('It is warm'), and she uttered the word 'mother' for the first time in her life.

"All that she touched inspired her, and yet what was most notable about Helen's breakthrough was what she did not touch and yet knew nonetheless. She seemed to have a profound 'grasp' of phenomena she never encountered or experienced. She spoke of sounds 'heard' and colors 'seen.' How could this be? How could she speak of or grasp the concepts of elements beneath the earth's surface? How could she have claimed knowledge of places never visited? How could she understand seemingly abstract concepts like love or thought? How could it be that a phenomenon, such as language—normally that we comprehend as being auditory and visual—be acquired chiefly by means of tactile sensation? How could Helen learn so much, and all through her hands and the tips of her fingers?

"There are several oddities about Helen's initiation into language that have important implications for our discussion: Helen was seven years old when she entered language. She claimed to have no memory of anything prior to that moment. All of her stories of previous moments were those told to her later in life by family and friends. She had no personal sense of identity prior to this moment. In later writings she referred to herself as 'Phantom.' After this moment, she had an immediate sense of conscious identity. She learned she had a father and a mother, a home, family who loved her, and she learned that everything has a 'name.' She learned that she had a name: H-e-l-e-n. She described her thoughts in terms of hand-sensations. All that she touched she integrated into her mind through the act of naming. Through this act she knew and had no problem with abstract concepts, such as love and thought, and through reading, she comprehended as well as anyone those objects, places, and people she had never seen, met, or experienced in person.

"In the Afterward to the most recent publishing of *Helen Keller's Autobiography, The Story of My Life,* Roger Shattuck observes:

> We soon learn how intimately Helen came to know plants and animals. She had no trouble believing in the reality of iron and coal in the ground, though she had never touched them . . . John Macy marveled at an 'inner faculty' that allowed Helen to reconstruct her visual and aural surroundings from another person's verbal account. Helen herself used the word 'imagination.' She would have welcomed T.S. Eliot's phrase 'the truth is in the imagination.'

"Nevertheless, there were skeptics who would not believe that her language was authentic but only parroted the words of others. Their worst suspicions were considered confirmed with the 'Frost King' plagiarism incident in which in one of the installments of her autobiography for the *Ladies' Home Journal*, she told a story from her youth in which it appeared that she plagiarized certain lines from a story she apparently never read. Only after the incident occurred did her mother realize that just before the onset of her illness she had read the 'plagiarized' passage to the toddler, Helen, who somehow called it forth from the depths of distant memory. The skeptics believed this to be evidence that the words she used were not really her own, but that she was in fact being fed these words by Sullivan and others. In a short time, however, she was vindicated.

"Helen's experiences in the initiation into language, along with the short-lived accusations of plagiarism, set up for us the paradox that is human language. *Syntax* deals with word order or sentence structure, whereas *semantics* deals with word usage or dictionary definitions. The novelist Walker Percy also considers *semiotics*, which for him consists of the question of *how* we understand one another, for the symbols of language become the signals of communication. According to Percy, the appearance of human language is most unprecedented in the history of the known universe. While dogs and other animals communicate through the use of signs and signals and sounds and sniffs, no other animal sits down to talk about work and play, relationships and dreams, and the multifarious stuff of human existence. Even in an everyday conversation, how humans communicate to understand one another is the single greatest mystery of humanity, which even finds paradigmatic form in the anomalous case of Helen Keller.

"It is true that the words that Helen Keller used were not 'truly' her own, but then neither are most of the words we use. We cannot communicate without words, and we must be given words by our parents and by the larger language communities into which we are born. In that sense, there is truly nothing new under the sun. Nevertheless, our own individual uniqueness and the singular circumstances through which we experience the use of these words and integrate them into our minds transform the words once belonging to others into our very own.

"Old words, however, do not necessarily imply old concepts recycled and imposed again and again, so that instead of a clear window into something new, we are left with a mirror of who we were before. We can, in fact, see the new along with the old, and in fact we must have the old in order to recognize the new for what it truly is in and of itself. This is where we find the splendor of language. This is what indicates there must be something more to cognition than reprocessing what we already know. There must be something else reprocessing and recycling the old, but only this time, into an entirely new configuration correlating with an entirely new experience, an entirely new insight into an aspect of a phenomenon previously unexplored. This gestalt is as miraculous as if we were to have ventured with the westward explorers of the 16th century to the boundaries of the known world, and then just as we crossed the border into the great unknown, the map suddenly sprang into action and began lightly tracing the contours of the surrounding terrain. It was surely not the map itself that performed this miracle of its own power, but rather something outside acting upon the map itself, only now in the mind of the explorer. Here, the explorer feels the tug in the depths of himself toward a particular direction, and if he heeds this directing, he might fare safely and successfully in his voyage.

"Likewise, we find ourselves taking a useful, if not an already used, map for gathering information on the terrain of our lives, but only this time we find ourselves in seemingly complex territory. Now we find ourselves not merely out upon and over a landscape, but ever inward, as well, in what we might call an 'inscape,' to use the term as Hopkins did. By 'inscape' he meant 'the unified complex of characteristics that give each thing its uniqueness and that differentiate it from other things,' and adding to this the term 'instress' or 'the force of being which holds the inscape together or the impulse from the inscape which carries it whole into the mind of the beholder.' Just as our outward five senses discern an external set of qualities around and between and linking the material objects in our world, so also do we have a mode of perceiving the complex of relationships that present to us the uniqueness of these various objects in their own inherently real way. These two concepts point to an ontological depth of being that resides as the relational substructure that tells us that there is so much more within and beyond ourselves than sense data images presented to the mind.

"That of which Hopkins wrote has important implications for explaining the kind of experience shared by Helen Keller and Ann Sullivan. It could only have been the instress of being upon being that awakened the darkened mind of young Helen. It was the breathing of life anew from inscape to inscape that awakened the uniqueness of her very self, brought it back to the land of the living, and opened up an eternal world to her. There was something much more at play here than just communication (i.e., as transmission of signals through a linguistic medium). That was the story of Helen's life prior to her awakening. Had not Helen's life, as described by her and others, been much more than a long and wearisome groping around within darkness? What occurred between Helen Keller and Ann Sullivan was so much more than the clanging chorus of cacophony, which is to say, they encountered beyond words the human way of communicating by means of interpersonal connection and communion.

"To many, Helen Keller was a quack-doctor's freak show. But she learned to listen, even though she was deaf, and she learned to perceive, even though she was blind. Could she possibly have something, just something, to teach us here in the academy?"

Shema peered at the class and saw that some had perceived and some were perplexed. He departed, reminding them of his scheduled tutorial to discuss their questions.

Hear, O Israel, the Lord is our God, and you must love the Lord your God with all your heart and soul and strength (Deut. 6:4).

Shema Tutorial

As Addy, Incredulous, and other students met with Shema after his stunning lecture, he playfully asked them, "Anything on your mind?"

"You must be psychic!" blurted out Addy.

"I don't know about being psychic," he retorted. "I just know about listening. God himself instructed Israel, 'Hear, O Israel: The Lord our God is One.'"

"You don't have to introduce a *deus ex machina* to resolve philosophical conundrums," replied Incredulous. "God is a projection of human wishes, of what we want but isn't really there."

"You seem suspicious of it all," perceived Shema, "but perhaps you long for a sense of something else, but you can't put your finger on it. There's a better way to learn and to listen. When you say you are skeptical, it sounds as if the current state of things is unacceptable to you, which means that there might be a better way, but you're not sure. Have you become so embedded in doubt that you can't indulge in some healthy skepticism toward . . ."

"Doubt!" Incredulous interjected. "That's a very good question." He felt provoked and a bit agitated. He wondered if Shema were toying with him.

"Good, you saw it for yourself! Are you prepared to question your own questions?" Shema probed as gently as he could.

"This is big stuff for me to reconsider," admitted Incredulous, "that there might actually be more rationality and regularity to the universe than I thought."

"There is always more to life than we can possibly conceptualize," responded Shema, "including patterns amidst chaos and confusion. Did you not just complete my sentence only a moment ago?"

"Yes," Incredulous agreed, "but I think you set me up for that one!"

"I confess to being a provocateur," Shema said, but the point is that you could recognize a logical conclusion, despite the unsettling reality that it causes you to question your own assumptions."

"Yes," replied Incredulous, but that's at the micro-level of our everyday lives. It tells us nothing about how the macro-level, or big picture, functions."

"Patience now, let it happen," counseled Shema. "You need to start with yourself before 'figuring out' the whole universe!"

The strangest thing to Incredulous was not that he was talking deeply and personally with a virtual stranger, but that he might have spent much of his life denying a larger rhyme and reason—a "something else," as Shema had phrased it—to life that he really thought did not exist. And that was disconcerting.

"That's right!" announced Addy. "There's gotta be something more to life than this. My God . . ."

"Yes," professed Berea, a fellow student who hadn't spoken up yet, "God. The only 'something else' that will satisfy our human longings is the God of the Bible. Read the Scriptures," he exhorted the group, "and you will find ultimate answers to perennial questions. Enough of all this circular questioning! It's wracking my brain!" he complained. "Sorry, I . . . uh . . . it's that this is all so overwhelming. And the Bible warns about listening to vain philosophies."

"Agreed, but reading—whether one is reading the Bible, philosophy, people, or whatever—presupposes the capacity to listen," noted Shema, "to set aside as far as humanly possible one's presuppositions and experiences to hear others speak on their own terms. Ancient Israel and the early church," he queried Berea, "both had to be open to new experiences to learn anew from God, did they not? Otherwise, we find ourselves in the everyday rut of the vanity of life itself that Ecclesiastes bemoans. Consider Moses at the burning bush or Saul on the road to Damascus, both of whom responded to God's self-revelation to them with the open-ended question, 'Who art thou?'

"Knowing presupposes listening," Shema summarized. "Listening is what I enjoy doing the most. And forgive me if I'm jumping ahead too fast, but this point is really my starting point: we must all listen to reality, which is to say, that which is outside of us but speaks to us and questions our facile assumptions and unbending ideologies."

"I'm very confused," confessed another student while others nodded their heads in agreement.

"As, no doubt, you should be," Shema replied, but then quickly added, "which is a good place to begin, if one seeks to be open, to listen to reality, to hear a penetrating question that probes deeply into our soul. Let me ask you this, How do you know your family, friends, and others whom you love and trust?

"I see what you mean," Addy acknowledged. "I know my best friends because we have experiences together. We trust each other, confide in each other, and even know what the other is thinking at times!"

"But that still doesn't mean that we can take that to the macro-level and explain it all that way," insisted Incredulous. "Things aren't always what they seem, you know, and one can't even always trust one's friends!"

"But we still must trust," Shema said with the confidence and assurance of someone who knew what he believed. "That's what you must do when you get to know your friends more deeply. You forget about the hows and whys of it all and spontaneously and reflexively respond with trust. And based on personal knowledge of another, you learn, you intuit whether to continue to grant your trust. But you must start with faith, if you wish to have friends!"

"I see, I think," Incredulous said as he almost felt a rare sense of calm.

"We know more than we can tell," Shema said. Then he added, "We know before we know." He quoted his favorite philosopher Sonorous Maximus:

> You always knew from the very beginning, you just didn't know how or why, or in what way. But you never stopped listening. And you were never quite satisfied. You were always asking questions, and not just for the sake of being difficult, but because you were looking for something. Even when you ran out of questions, and words to go with them, you never stopped asking. And yet you did not give up until it hit, until it came through as the rain. And just as rain clears away all things, so it has here and now, and so it will continue. So now, here you are. And you're right. And you've been right all along!

And though Addy could not comprehend fully the magnitude of their discussion, she heard and knew of what Shema said about personal knowledge. She thought of her so-called friends with whom she did drugs, and she finally realized she had been evading life's challenges and questions. "I'm beginning to see more clearly now, but it's still so puzzling. Why did it take all this time for me to open my eyes?"

"When you hear an answer, which you consider real and true," Shema observed in acknowledgement of her moment of realization, "please tell me so I too may hear."

To agree without understanding is inane. To disagree without understanding is impudent.

Φ M. Adler

Appendix on Mortimore Mortimer Adler Contributions to Intelligent Reading

Reading books, for Adler, is a personal matter! The skillful reading of a book is like the personal discussions between close friends who understand each other. Adler asks us to sit down, be a bit imaginative, and proceed as though we were sitting down face-to-face with the writer in person; the intimacy is analogous to a personal discussion with a friend.

Adler emphasizes the importance of reading the author's writings, or primary sources (in contrast to commentaries, or secondary resources, written by others to further evaluate and explain the life and work of the author in question). For example, we must read Aristotle to understand his philosophy and how it may or may not be relevant to our lives. Secondary sources may be useful references for points of interpretation, but ultimately we ought to listen primarily to the author's own words. Therefore, Adler implores that we sit down and wrestle with the author "face-to-face" to seek understanding of his or her intended message and how it might affect our lives and worldviews today.

Adler urges us to come to terms with what the author wishes to say. This process involves a form of listening by close and active reading, noting patterns of words, writing style, and key concepts. Such close reading involves careful consideration of each word, and here a dictionary and thesaurus are helpful, as many words are used in a variety of ways that do not always correspond to the informal usage of daily living. Furthermore, methods of underlining and noting questions and comments in the margins contribute to such understanding (see specific suggestions at the end of this Appendix on reading and marking up a book).

After having come to terms with the author, readers are then in position to consider their responses to the author's message. Do they agree or disagree, and why? What are the most convincing or unconvincing elements of the author's viewpoint, and how could they be strengthened, altered, or challenged? For Adler, it is the call and the response, the back and forth of dialogue, the heckling and haggling of Socrates in the agora, that is the process by which we come to have knowledge of truth (be it regarding the essential nature of the cosmos, the purpose[s] of our lives, or why it was that my girlfriend said only two words to me the whole way in the car during the four-hour trip to her mother's house).

Getting Personal Now: How to Read a Book

Let's pause now and suspend all disbelief for a moment. Imagine that a close friend is sitting before you now requesting your undivided attention for a while to discuss a matter of utmost importance to her. She requests that you bear with her and listen to her whole story, and she hopes that you will offer her feedback that will be of use to her in her crisis. How would you respond? Would you make time? Of course you would! You would listen intently and hope that your experience would be sufficient to aid her in whatever difficulty she may be experiencing. Because you are close friends, it would not be too difficult to listen with empathy and to be able to understand what she is trying to communicate. Then, on the basis of an accurate understanding of her crisis, it is hoped that you would offer a helpful response.

Let's say now that your friend is not experiencing a crisis of life or death proportions but, rather, has stumbled across what she considers to be a great idea, one that she wishes to share with you because she trusts you and values the thoughtfulness of your opinions. So it is a joyful sharing of a new discovery, and you wish to understand her viewpoint as fully as possible.

Adler has a set of guidelines that may be helpful in such a situation. The first step involves the suspension of judgment for a moment while your friend is speaking. Allow her to discuss fully her proposition. This does not mean that you agree or that you simply surrender your thoughts as though they had no importance. It simply means you withhold your assessment of her discovery until she has had an opportunity to explain it as completely and clearly as possible. As she is speaking, attempt to "try on"—just as in a clothing store—her point of view for a moment. In a clothing store, taking a shirt back to the dressing rooms does not necessitate buying the shirt but is rather postponing the decision of whether or not to buy it until you have tried it on. In the same way, take your friend's perspective back to the changing room of your mind and wear it around a little, if only for the duration of her explanation. The point is that the attempt to understand her from her own perspective will enable you to be of greater help to her in your forthcoming feedback, and ultimately it will prove to be decisive in the continuation and deepening of your friendship.

Next, engage in active listening. During the course of her discussion, stop her for a moment to summarize what she has said in the form of a question. Such questions might begin with, "Do I understand that you mean . . . ?" This helps your friend to know you are listening, and it clarifies each party's thinking and understanding, preparing the way for a thoughtful response. You might also find that, though you thought you understood, you had, in actuality, misinterpreted her words. You feel comfortable clarifying your thinking, and she feels at ease because you are not attempting to undermine hers. Limit interruptions only to ask questions, not to impose your opinions or aim to change hers. Such interruptions to seize control may do more harm than good and close off future opportunities to offer your guidance and service to her as a friend.

Once your friend has finished her explanation and you have asked all pertinent questions so as to understand her position thoroughly, then it is your turn to offer your response or perspective. Such a perspective should avoid any form of arrogance. If you agree with her completely, do not validate her ideas as though your agreement were necessary for their validity. If you disagree with her to any degree, first explain clearly and specifically what about her viewpoint, in its assumptions, methods, and conclusions, is particularly strong, and then offer what you think needs to be strengthened.

The chief point is that no matter what conclusions you draw about her decisions, your response to her and the expression of your thoughts should always take the form of open-minded listening and speaking that maintains a respectful relationship between you as both the primary end and the means through which you both arrive at knowledge.

In these preceding paragraphs, we have seen in the form of a hypothetical encounter with a close friend, Adler's general approach to reading a book. We have the personal encounter with the friend and the process of coming to terms with the friend's way of thinking, which set the stage for a meeting of minds. Adler views the reading of books in analogous fashion. He offers specific points for intelligent reading with an overall purpose of understanding an author:

I. Skim or pre-read the book, examining the title page, preface and introduction, table of contents, index, and publisher's blurb to obtain an overall idea of the book's thesis, topics, and structure.

II. A more careful inspection will include discerning the overall theme of the book, details and arguments of the thesis, and an assessment of the significance and truth of the book. Specific techniques of marking a book include underlining of key points (or vertical lines in the margin for lengthy passages), stars or asterisks for crucial points or summary statements, circling and defining of key terms, and writing numbers, comments, or questions to outline and probe more deeply the argument.

III. A deeper analytical reading of the book will understand the book as a whole (subject matter and genre, brief statement of its thesis, outline of the argument, and a definition of the author's aim); the book in details (understanding key terms, propositions, arguments, and a determination of how and whether the author has successfully accomplished his goal); and criticism based on a careful understanding of the author and not mere personal reaction (specifically saying why one agrees and why one disagrees, including an evaluation of the author's strengths and weaknesses in terms of information, logic, and helpfulness).

Concluding observations

Do you have questions? Be specific and try to put into words the questions you have about the author's argument and your response to it. What do you think? What is your response? Summarize your own thoughts about the work in question based on a careful understanding of the author's purpose, thesis, and argumentation.

Cast of Characters
(In Order of Appearance)

Addy: a troubled seeker who has become open to greater meaning in life beyond addiction to drugs, peers, and fads.

Shema (Hebrew word for "hear"): foundational Jewish confession of faith (Deut. 6:4).

Sonorous Maximus: one who hears greatly.

Univocal: a traditional realist (cf. M. Adler) who affirms a one-to-one correspondence between meaning and reality.

Equivocal: a postmodern deconstructionist (cf. J. Derrida) who affirms multiple meanings and interpretations of reality.

Incredulous: an uncommitted skeptic.

Harmonious: a critically realist theologian (cf. T. F. Torrance) who believes in harmony, whether musical or epistemological.

Cacophonous: a postmodernist philosopher (cf. J-F. Lyotard) who affirms the dissonance of loud and noisy, even if, "unpleasant" sounds.

Berea: a city of Macedonia to which the Apostle Paul preaches and in which those who hear his sermons search the Scriptures for themselves to judge the veracity of his message.

Bibliography

Mortimer J. Adler:

How to Read a Book: The Classic Guide to Intelligent Reading, rev. ed. with Charles van Doren (NY: Touchstone, 1972).

How to Speak, How to Listen (NY: Collier, 1983).

Intellect: Mind Over Matter (NY: Collier, 1990).

Ten Philosophical Mistakes: Basic Errors in Modern Thought—How They Came About, Their Consequences, and How to Avoid Them (NY: Macmillan, 1985).

Albert Einstein:

Ideas and Opinions (NY: Dell, reprinted by Crown, 1978).

The World As I See It (NY: Citadel, 1984).

Peggy Kamuf (ed.):

A Derrida Reader: Between the Blinds (NY: Columbia, 1991).

James Loder & W. Jim Neidhardt:

The Knight's Move: The Relational Logic of the Spirit in Theology and Science (Colorado Springs: Helmers & Howard, 1992).

Jean-François Lyotard:

The Postmodern Condition: A Report on Knowledge, tr. G. Bennington & B. Massumi (Minneapolis, MN: Univ. of Minn. Pr., 1979).

Jacob Needlemam:

The Heart of Philosophy (NY: Harper & Row, 1982).

Walker Percy:

The Message in the Bottle: How Queer Man Is, How Queer Language Is, and What One Has to Do with the Other (NY: Noonday Press, 1954).

The Moviegoer (NY: Fawcett, 1961).

Michael Polanyi:

Personal Knowledge: Towards a Post-Critical Philosophy (Chicago: Univ. of Chicago Press, 1962).

Richard Rorty, http://www.stanford.edu/~rrorty:

"Analytic Philosophy and Transformative Philosophy"

"The Decline of Redemptive Truth and the Rise of a Literary Culture"

"A Pragmatist View of Contemporary Analytic Philosophy"

"Redemption from Egotism: James and Proust as Spiritual Exercises"

Also, "Introduction: Metaphilosophical Difficulties of Linguistic Philosophy," *The Linguistic Turn: Recent Essays in Philosophical Method* (Chicago: Univ. of Chicago Press, 1967)

Stuart Sim, ed.:

The Routledge Companion to Postmodernism (NY: Routledge, 2001)

Robert C. Solomon:

A Short Introduction to Philosophy, 4th ed. (NY: Harcourt Brace, 1994).

Thomas F. Torrance:

Belief in Science and in Christian Life: The Relevance of Michael Polanyi's Thought for Christian Life and Thought (Edinburgh: Handsel Press, 1980).

Reality and Scientific Theology (Edinburgh: Scottish Academic Press, 1985).

Theological Science (London: Oxford Univ. Press, 1969).

Transformation and Convergence in the Frame of Knowledge: Explorations in the Interrelations of Scientific and Theological Enterprise (Grand Rapids: Eerdmans Pub. Co., 1984).